STARTING
TECHNOLOGY

WATER

John Williams

Illustrated by
Malcolm S. Walker

Wayland

Titles in this series

AIR
TIME
WATER
WHEELS

Words printed in **bold** appear in the glossary on page 30

© Copyright 1990 Wayland (Publishers) Ltd

First published in 1990 by
Wayland (Publishers) Ltd
61 Western Road, Hove
East Sussex BN3 1JD, England

This edition published in 1991 by
Wayland (Publishers) Ltd

Editor: Anna Girling
Designer: Kudos Design Services

British Library Cataloguing in Publication Data
Williams, John
  Water.
  1. Water
  I. Title II. Series
  553.7

ISBN 1 85210 923 8 **Hardback**
ISBN 0 7502 0270 X **Paperback**

Typeset by Kudos Editorial and Design Services, Sussex, England
Printed in Italy by Rotolito Lombarda S.p.A.
Bound in Belgium by Casterman S.A.

CONTENTS

Floating   4

More Floating   6

Why Things Float   8

Rafts   10

Longboats   12

Boat Shapes   14

Paddle Boats   16

Jet Boats   18

More About Sails   20

Propellers   22

Submarines   24

Fish   26

Notes for Parents and Teachers   28

Glossary   30

Books to Read   31

Index   32

FLOATING

Some things float and some things sink. It does not matter how large or small they are. Big, heavy things can float, while very small things may sink.

Very large boats like this one take big, heavy loads all over the world.

Testing for floaters and sinkers

You will need:

A washing-up bowl filled with water
A piece of card or paper
Felt tip pens

1. Find twenty objects made from as many different **materials** as possible. Rubber, wood, metal and plastic objects are good to try.

2. Draw two circles on the piece of card. Make the circles overlap. Label one circle 'Floaters' and the other 'Sinkers'.

3. Test each of your twenty objects to see if they float or sink in the bowl of water. Write the name of each object in the 'Floaters' or 'Sinkers' circles.

4. Test your floaters again. Do they always float or can you make them sink? Try pushing them under the water. Do they sink or bob up again? Do they fill with water and then sink? List any floaters that you could make sink in the overlapping part of your two circles.

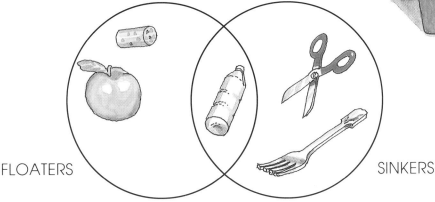

FLOATERS   SINKERS

MORE FLOATING

Making kitchen foil boats

You will need:

Kitchen foil
Scissors
Plasticine
A bowl of water
Weighing scales

1. Cut out some sheets of kitchen foil and make some simple boats. Experiment with several shapes. They should all be about 15 cm long and 10 cm wide. Make sure they do not leak.

2. Float the boats on the water. Gently fill them with little pieces of plasticine until they sink.

3. Weigh the amounts of plasticine in each boat. Did all the boats hold the same amount of plasticine?

4. Weigh one of the boats without its plasticine. How much lighter is it than the plasticine that was in it?

Making a plasticine boat

You will need:

Plasticine
A rolling pin
A bowl of water
Marbles

1. Take the plasticine which you used to sink one of your kitchen foil boats. Roll out the plasticine until it is thin. Make it into a simple boat.

2. Gently lower your boat on to the water. When it is floating properly, carefully fill it with marbles, one at a time. Count how many marbles it will hold before it sinks.

WHY THINGS FLOAT

Fill a basin with water. Try to hold a block of wood under the water. Can you feel the wood pushing upwards? It is this upward push that helps objects float.

These big logs float. The men are able to stand on them on the water.

Experimenting with floating

You will need:

A bucket of water
A brick
String
A spring balance
Plasticine

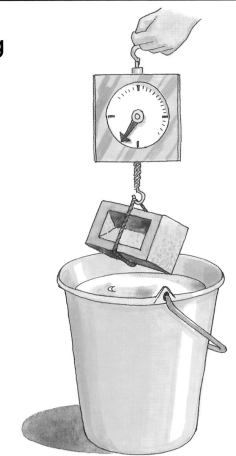

1. Tie the string to the brick and hang it from the spring balance. Gently lower it into the water. Look to see what happens to the reading on the balance.

2. Do the same experiment with a ball of plasticine. Like the brick, it appears to weigh less when it is lowered into the water.

3. Now roll out the plasticine and shape it into a boat. Hang it from the spring balance and lower it into the water. See what happens to the reading on the balance this time.

RAFTS

Long ago, people made rafts for travelling on water. Rafts are floating platforms made of logs or planks fixed together.

People also hollowed out tree trunks to make **canoes**. These canoes rolled over easily, so people fitted **outriggers** on the sides. Even today, some **yachts** use this idea to stop them tipping over in the water.

These are modern canoes used for sport.

Making rafts

You will need:

Corks
Rubber bands
Lollipop sticks

1. Make a simple raft by fixing two corks together with rubber bands.

2. To make a larger raft, fix some lollipop sticks across the corks to give support.

3. Float your rafts on some water.

Making an outrigger

1. Make a model man out of pipe cleaners. Sit him on your twig 'boat' on some water. See if you can stop him rolling over.

2. Use three manicure sticks to make an outrigger for your twig 'boat'. Fix the sticks and the twig in a square with a rubber band at each corner.

You will need:

Pipe cleaners
A thick, straight
  twig
Wooden
  manicure sticks
  (you can buy
  these from a
  chemist's shop)
Four rubber
  bands

3. Put your model man on your boat now. Does it roll over?

LONGBOATS

Longboats were used hundreds of years ago by the **Vikings**. The Vikings were famous for their sea journeys. They often sailed hundreds of miles in very bad weather. They even sailed across the Atlantic Ocean from Europe to America in their longboats.

This is a model of a Viking longboat. It has a small sail and lots of oars. Count how many oars you can see.

Making a model longboat

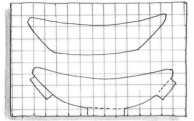

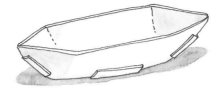

Card
Pencils
Scissors
Paper glue
A wooden
  manicure stick
Paints

1. Cut the two sides of the **hull** from a large piece of card. On one of the sides include three small flaps. It helps to draw the shapes on squared paper first.

2. Glue the flaps and stick the two sides of the hull together.

Mast

3. Cut out the other parts of the boat from the card. You will need a sail, seats, oars, one steering oar, a **figurehead** and a flag.

Sail

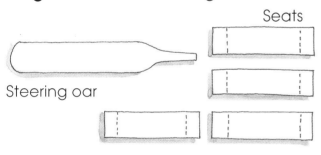

Seats

Steering oar

Oars

4. Glue all these parts to the hull. Use the manicure stick as the **mast**.

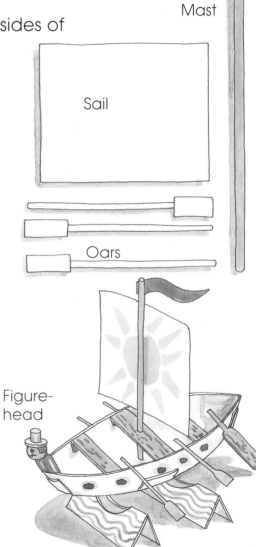

Figure-
head

5. Cut out two squares of card to make a stand for your longboat. Fold them in half and cut a hole in the middle for the boat to sit in.

6. Decorate the boat with paints.

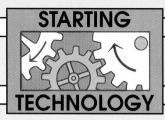
BOAT SHAPES

Making balsawood boats

You will need:

A sheet of balsawood
  about 3-5 mm thick
A junior hacksaw
Thin card

Scissors
Wooden
  manicure sticks
A straw

> **WARNING:** When cutting balsawood, always use a junior hacksaw. Try not to breathe in any sawdust. Ask an adult to help you if you need to use a knife.

1. Cut out some simple boats, about 12 cm long, from the wood. Each boat should have a different **bow**.

2. Cut out some triangles and squares from the card. These will be the sails.

3. Use the manicure sticks as masts. Thread them through the sails and fix them to the boats.

4. Float your boats on some water. Blow on the back of the sails through the straw. Which boat shape works best? Which sail shape works best?

5. Fix your best sail to your best boat. Do these two together work best of all?

Making keels and rudders

You will need:

Some thin plastic
Scissors

1. Use thin plastic from a food container. Cut out a **keel** and a **rudder**.

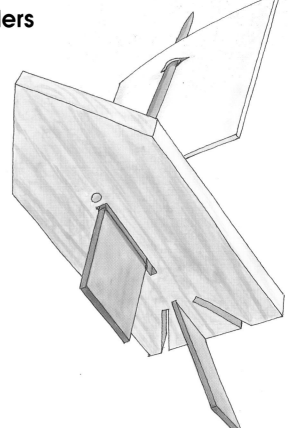

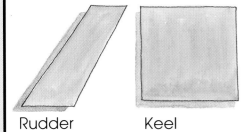

Rudder   Keel

2. Cut a slot in the middle of your balsawood boat, big enough for your keel. The keel will help keep the boat upright and stop it from being blown sideways.

3. Cut three slots in the **stern** of the boat. Slide your rudder into one of the slots.

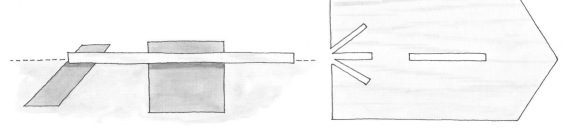

4. Float your boat on some water. Put the rudder in different slots. Which direction does it take?

PADDLE BOATS

Paddle wheels can be used to make boats move along on the water. Have you ever been on a pedalo on a boating lake? Pedalos are small boats with paddle wheels. The wheel goes round when you turn the pedals.

Old paddle boats like this one in the USA take tourists on river trips.

Making a paddle boat

You will need:

Balsawood
A junior hacksaw
A strong rubber band
A stapler

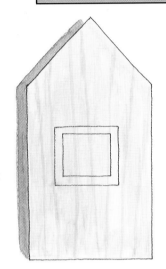

1. Cut out a boat shape from the balsawood.

2. Cut a square piece out of the centre of the boat. This piece will be the paddle.

3. Make the square piece smaller so that it will fit into the hole in the centre of the boat with room to spare.

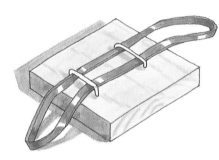

4. Fix the centre of the rubber band to the paddle with a staple. Staple the ends of the band to the boat.

5. Wind up the rubber band by turning the paddle. Lower the boat on to some water and let the paddle go.

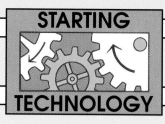

JET BOATS

Making a jet boat

You will need:

Balsawood
A junior hacksaw
A balloon
Scissors

Narrow plastic tubing
Sticky tape
A strong rubber band

1. Cut out a balsawood boat.

2. Cut the lip off the balloon.

3. Stretch the mouth of the balloon over the end of a short piece of plastic tubing. Fix the balloon to the tube with sticky tape.

4. Blow up the balloon. Slide the end of the tube under a rubber band at the back of the boat. You may lose some of the air as you are doing this!

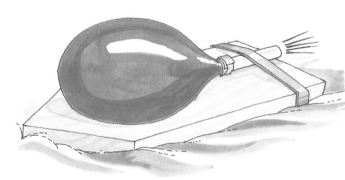

5. Put the boat on some water and let the air go.

Further work

Make plastic keels and rudders like the ones on page 15 for your paddle boat and jet boat. Fix a rudder to the front of one of your boats. Does this work as well as the rudder at the back does?

Speed boats can go very fast. They make jets of water which push them along.

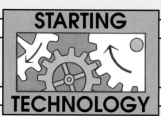
MORE ABOUT SAILS

There are two main kinds of sailing boat. Long ago, many big sailing boats had sails that went across the boat. These were called square-riggers. Smaller boats, like modern yachts, usually have a fore-and-aft sail, which means it goes from the front to the back of the boat.

Look at all these racing yachts. Many of them have big extra sails called spinnakers at the front to make them go faster.

Making a sailing boat

You will need:

Two plastic
  bottles
Garden canes
Rubber bands
Tissue paper
Scissors
Cotton thread
Sticky tape

1. Fix the two plastic bottles together using the garden canes and rubber bands.

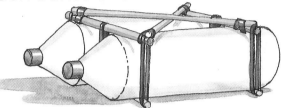

2. Cut out a triangle from tissue paper to make a fore-and-aft sail.

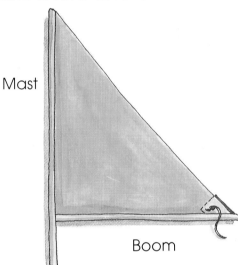

Mast

Boom

3. Use garden canes as a mast and **boom** and fix the sail to them with sticky tape.

4. Stick a short length of cotton thread to the corner of the sail.

5. Attach the mast to the middle of your boat. Stick the free end of the thread to the end of the boat. Test your boat on some water.

6. Make a square-rigger sail in the same way. Attach it to your boat instead of the fore-and-aft sail. Which works best?

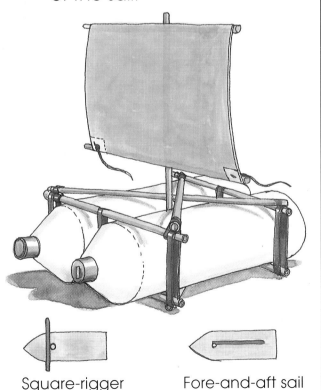

Square-rigger   Fore-and-aft sail

PROPELLERS

A propeller has blades which spin round and push a boat along on the water. You can make a propeller unit to fit on your plastic bottle boat (see page 21) instead of a sail.

Propellers like this one drive the biggest ships and oil tankers.

Making a propeller unit

You will need:

A stiff plastic tube
A bead
A nail
A cork
A metal
  paperclip
A strong rubber
  band
A model plastic
  propeller

1. Buy a piece of stiff plastic tube, about 25 cm long, from a do-it-yourself shop.

2. Straighten out the paperclip, leaving a hook at one end.

3. Thread the clip through the cork, then the bead and finally the propeller. Bend the straight end of the clip tightly over the propeller.

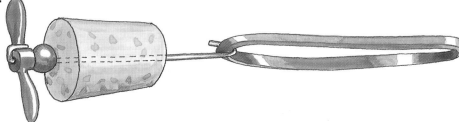

4. Attach the rubber band to the hook at the other end of the paperclip. Pass the rubber band through the plastic tube. Use the nail to hold the band at the other end.

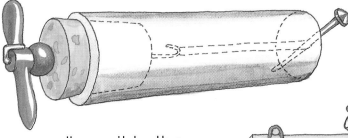

5. Fix the propeller unit to the back of your boat.

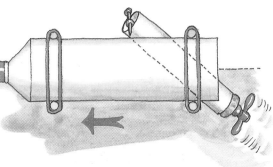

6. Wind up the propeller. Put the boat on some water and let the propeller go.

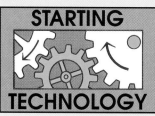

SUBMARINES

We often need to know what is at the bottom of the sea. People may need to go deep into the water to build bridges or lay pipes. If they need to go very deep they use **submarines**.

This huge submarine can stay under the water for many weeks at a time.

Making a model submarine

You will need:

A glass bottle
A rubber bung with two holes in it
Plastic tubing
A large bowl of water

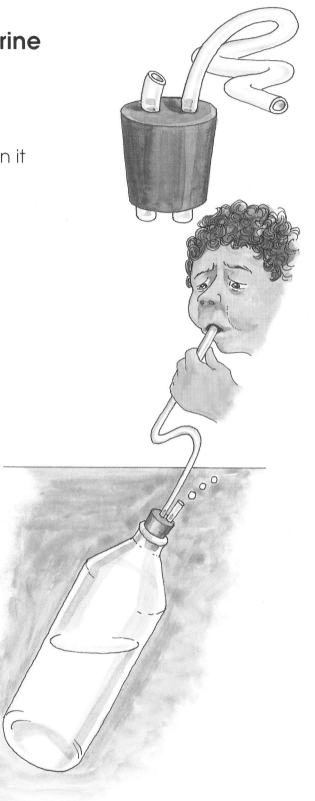

1. Push plastic tubes through the two holes in the bung. One should be a long piece of tubing and the other quite short.

2. Push the bung firmly into the neck of the bottle.

3. Put the bottle in the bowl and let it fill with water through the short tube.

4. Now blow through the long tube. Some of the water will be pushed out of the other hole in the bung and the bottle will rise.

5. Put your finger over the end of the long tube. The air will stay in your 'submarine'. What happens when you take your finger off the end of the tube?

FISH

Fish live in water. Most fish have **fins** which help them balance and move in the water. If you have an **aquarium** at school or at home, look to see how the fish use their fins. Do they move their fins all the time?

There are lots of fish in this aquarium. Look at the shape and size of their fins.

Making a food chain mobile

Many different kinds of plants, fish and other animals live in water. Some fish eat the tiny plants and animals in the water. Some big fish catch and eat small fish. A food chain shows how this works.

You will need:

Card
Scissors
Felt tip pens
String

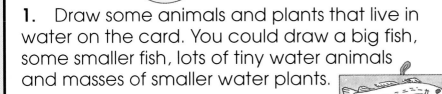

1. Draw some animals and plants that live in water on the card. You could draw a big fish, some smaller fish, lots of tiny water animals and masses of smaller water plants.

2. Cut out your pictures and string them together. Put them in the order of the food chain.

3. The fish at the top of the mobile needs large amounts of small animals and plants for its food. So the largest card must be at the bottom.

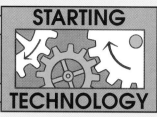

SCIENCE

This book is concerned essentially with simple technology, but it also attempts to explain the basic science of floating and sinking. Children find it difficult to understand why solid metal objects — such as scissors — sink, while a large metal boat floats. They will accept that solid wood floats, but not understand why.

It is not good enough simply to talk about the air inside a floating object. After all, children will wonder how much air there can be in a fully-laden oil tanker — yet it still floats. The concept of density is far too abstract for young children, and it would be a mistake to introduce it at this stage. However, by allowing them to experiment with a sequence of objects that float or sink — foil, plasticine or marbles — children can be given the opportunity to understand that virtually all materials will float, given the right conditions. Children should also experience the 'push' of water and be introduced to the forces which keep things afloat.

DESIGN AND TECHNOLOGY

Making the models in this book will involve many aspects of design and technology. After experimenting with the basic models, children should be encouraged to make a better design in the light of what they have learned. In this way children will be acquiring important technological skills. They will learn to identify problems and use their scientific knowledge to devise ways of solving them.

LANGUAGE

The topic of water will provide a wealth of opportunities for children to extend their language skills. The science of floating and sinking and the various designs of boats and rafts will give rise to much discussion. There will also be opportunities for written work — both creative writing and the factual reporting of experiments.

MATHEMATICS

The measuring, timing and estimating involved in the activities in this book will give children the chance to use mathematics to solve practical problems.

WARNING: Teachers should be aware of the dangers to children caused by the misuse of tools, especially those with a cutting edge. However, the boats shown in this book only need the most basic implements, such as a small hacksaw and a pair of scissors.

National Curriculum Attainment Targets

This book is relevant to the following Attainment Targets in the National Curriculum for science:

Attainment Target 1 (Exploration of science)   The designing, making and testing of all the boats throughout the book, and the various experiments with floating and sinking, answer many of the requirements of this Attainment Target.

Attainment Target 10 (Forces)   The forces involved in floating and sinking are listed in this Attainment Target. Work on floating and sinking, rafts, boat designs and submarines is relevant. Forces are also included in work on sailing boats.

Attainment Target 13 (Energy)   Activities such as making paddle boats, jet boats and propellers involve simple mechanisms which can store energy and change it into movement. Sails transfer energy from the wind into movement. The discussion of energy is also relevant to work on the food chain in the final chapter.

The following Attainment Targets are included to a lesser extent:

Attainment Target 2 (The variety of life) and **Attainment Target 3** (Processes of life)   Work on the food chain concerns the relationship between many different living things and shows that food is necessary for life.

Teachers should also be aware of the Attainment Targets covered in other National Curriculum documents — that is, those for technology and design, mathematics, history and language.

GLOSSARY

Aquarium A large glass container where fish are kept.

Boom A pole on a boat which holds the sail in the right place.

Bow The front of a boat.

Canoes Narrow boats that you move by using a paddle.

Figurehead A carved figure sometimes attached to the front of sailing ships long ago.

Fins The thin parts that stand out from the body of a fish and help it swim.

Hull The main shell of a boat.

Keel A long piece of wood or metal attached to the bottom of a boat.

Mast A tall pole which holds up the sail on a boat.

Materials Different substances that things can be made out of.

Outriggers Extra floats attached to the side of boats to help keep them upright.

Rudder A flat piece of wood or metal attached to the end of a boat and used to steer it.

Stern The back of a boat.

Submarines Boats that can travel under water.

Vikings People who lived in northern Europe about 1,000 years ago and went on long sea journeys.

Yachts Sailing boats which can travel very fast.

BOOKS TO READ

Floating and Sinking   by Ed Catherall (Wayland, 1985)
Floating and Sinking   by Terry Jennings (Oxford University Press, 1988)
Life in the Water   by Keith Porter (Macmillan, 1986)
On the Water   by Julie Fitzpatrick (Hamish Hamilton, 1984)
Water   by Brenda Walpole (Kingfisher, 1987)

Picture acknowledgements
The publishers would like to thank the following for allowing their photographs to be reproduced in this book: Eye Ubiquitous 12; Tony Stone Worldwide 10 (Chris Cole), 19, 20 (Alastair Black); Zefa 4, 8, 16 (H Steenmans), 22, 24, 26 (C Voigt). Cover photography by Zul Mukhida.

America 12
aquariums 26
Atlantic Ocean 12

balsawood boats 14 - 15,
   17 - 18
booms 21

canoes 10

Europe 12

figureheads 13
fins 26
fish 26 - 7
floating 4 - 9
food chain mobile 27

hulls 13

jet boats 18 - 19

keels 15, 19
kitchen foil boats 6 - 7

logs 8, 10
longboats 12

masts 13 - 14, 21

oars 12 - 13
outriggers 10 - 11

paddle boats 16 - 17
pedalos 16
plastic bottle boats 21 - 3
plasticine boats 7, 9
propellers 22 - 3

rafts 10 - 11
rudders 15, 19

sailing boats 20 - 21
sails 12 - 14, 20 - 21
sinking 4 - 7
speed boats 19
square-riggers 20 - 21
sterns 15
submarines 24 - 5

USA 16

Vikings 12

yachts 10, 20